First published in Great Britain in 1996 by Brockhampton Press,
a member of the Hodder Headline Group, 20 Bloomsbury Street,
London WC1B 3QA.

This series of little gift books was made by Frances Banfield,
Kate Brown, Laurel Clark, Penny Clarke, Clive Collins, Melanie
Cumming, Nick Diggory, Deborah Gill, David Goodman, Douglas
Hall, Maureen Hill, Nick Hutchison, John Hybert, Kate Hybert,
Douglas Ingram, Simon London, Patrick McCreeth, Morse Modaberi,
Tara Neill, Anne Newman, Grant Oliver, Michelle Rogers,
Nigel Soper, Karen Sullivan and Nick Wells.

Compilation and selection copyright
© 1996 Brockhampton Press.

ISBN 1 86019 462 1

A copy of the CIP data is available from the
British Library upon request.

Produced for Brockhampton Press by Flame Tree Publishing,
part of The Foundry Creative Media Company Limited,
The Long House, Antrobus Road, Chiswick W4 5HY.

Printed and bound in Italy by L.E.G.O. Spa.

The Funny Book of
CATS

Words selected by
Bob Hale

Cartoons by
DOUGLAS INGRAM.

BROCKHAMPTON PRESS

'When in doubt – any kind of doubt – <u>Wash!</u>
That is Rule Number 1,' said Jennie.

Paul Gallico, **Jennie**

The Lion

The Lion, the Lion, he swells in the waste,
He has a big head and a very small waist;
But his shoulders are stark,
and his jaws they are grim,
And a good little child will not play with him.

The Tiger

The Tiger, on the other hand, is kittenish and mild,
He makes a pretty playfellow for any little child;
And mothers of large families
(who claim to common sense)
Will find a Tiger will repay the trouble and expense.

Hilaire Belloc

'Did you ever see the Catskill Mountains?'
'No, but I've seen them kill mice.'

Anonymous

Even overweight cats instinctively know the cardinal
rule: when fat, arrange yourself in slim poses.

John Weitz

There are people who reshape the world by
force or argument, but the cat just lies there,
dozing, and the world quietly reshapes itself
to suit his comfort and convenience.

Allen and Ivy Dodd

A cat allows you to sleep on the bed. On the edge.

Jenny De Vries

When I play with my cat, who knows if I
am not a pastime to her more than she is to me?

Montaigne

[Jeremy] Bentham was very fond of animals,
particularly 'pussies' as he called them, 'when they
had domestic virtues'; but he had no particular
affection for the common race of cats. He had
one, however, of which he used to boast that
he had 'made a man of him,' and whom
he was wont to invite to eat macaroni (sic)
at his own table. This puss got knighted, and
rejoiced in the name of Sir John Langborn.

John Bowring, **The Works of Jeremy Bentham**

At dinner time he would sit in a corner,
concentrating, and suddenly they would say,
'Time to feed the cat,' as if it was their own idea.

Lilian Jackson Braun

People meeting for the first time suddenly
relax if they find they both have cats.
And plunge into anecdote.

Charlotte Gray

Three tabbies took out their cats to tea,
As well-behaved tabbies as well could be:
Each sat in the chair that each preferred,
They mewed for their milk,
and they sipped and purred.
Now tell me this (as these cats you've seen them) -
How many lives had these cats between them?

*Kate Greenaway, **Three Tabbies***

Next to a wife whom I idolise, give me a cat.
Mark Twain

Nobody who is not prepared to spoil cats
will get from them the reward they are able
to give to those who do spoil them.
Compton Mackenzie

After scolding one's cat one looks into its face and
is seized by the ugly suspicion that it understood
every word. And has filed it for reference.
Charlotte Gray

Do you know why Cats always wash themselves after a meal? A Cat caught a sparrow and was about to devour it, but the sparrow said, 'No gentleman eats till he has first washed his face.' The Cat, struck with this remark, set the sparrow down, and began to wash his face with his paw, but the sparrow flew away. This vexed Pussy extremely, and he said, 'As long as I live, I will eat first and wash my face afterwards.' Which all cats do, even to this day.

Charles Ross, **The Book of Cats**

Confound the cats! All cats - alway -
Cats of all colours, black, white, grey;
By night a nuisance and by day -
Confound the cats!

Orlando Dobbin, **A Dithyramb on Cats**

Places to look: behind the books in the
bookshelf, any cupboard with a gap too small
for any cat to squeeze through, the top of
anything sheer, under anything too low for
a cat to squash under and inside the piano.

Roseanne Ambrose Brown

The cat sat asleep by the side of the fire,
    The mistress snored as loud as a pig;
Jack took up his fiddle by Jenny's desire,
    And struck up a bit of a jig.

Whimsical Incidents, 1805

Cats like doors left open - in case
they change their minds.
Rosemary Nisbet

One day a cat will join you while you are utterly
relaxed in muscle and brain, and with a delicate
miaow and a velvet paw will show you
transcendental meditation by an expert.
V. Martin

The saxophones wailed like melodious
cats under the moon.
Aldous Huxley, **Brave New World**

... More ways of killing a cat than
choking it with cream.

Charles Kingsley, **Westward Ho**

Another silence fell on the group, and then Miss
Resker, in her best district-visitor manner, asked if
the human language had been difficult to learn.
Tobermory looked squarely at her for a moment and
then fixed his gaze serenely on the middle distance.
It was obvious that boring questions
lay outside his scheme of life.
'What do you think of human intelligence?'
asked Mavis Pellington lamely.
'Of whose intelligence in particular?'
asked Tobermory coldly.
'Oh, well, of mine for instance,'
said Mavis, with a feeble laugh.
'You put me in an embarrassing position,' said
Tobermory, whose tone and attitude certainly did
not suggest a shred of embarrassment. 'When your

inclusion in this house-party was suggested Sir Wilfrid protested that you were the most brainless woman of his acquaintance, and that there was a wide distinction between hospitality and the care of the feeble-minded. Lady Blemley replied that your lack of brain-power was the precise quality which had earned you your invitation, as you were the only person she could think of who might be idiotic enough to buy their old car. You know, the one they call "The Envy of Sisyphus" because it goes quite nicely uphill if you push it.'

Lady Blemley's protestations would have had greater effect if she had not casually suggested to Mavis only that morning that the car in question would be just the thing for her down at her Devonshire home.

Saki, **Tobermory**

There is nothing so lowering to one's self-esteem
as the affectionate contempt of a beloved cat.
Monica Edwards

The world is so full of such edible things,
I'll nibble their feet, and I'll chew off their wings.
Henry Beard, **Catty Thoughts by
Robert Louis Stevenson's Cat**

The young alligator became so tame that it
followed him about the house like a dog,
scrambling up the stairs after him, and showing
much affection and docility. Its great favourite,
however, was a cat, and the friendship was mutual.
When the cat was reposing herself before the fire,
the alligator would lay himself down, place his
head upon the cat, and in this attitude go to sleep.
Edward Jesse, **Gleanings in Natural History**

When the tea is brought at five o' clock,
And all the neat curtains are drawn with care,
The little black cat with the bright green eyes,
Is suddenly purring there.
*Harold Monro, **Milk for the Cat***

Let Hercules himself do what he may,
The cat will mew and dog will have his day.
William Shakespeare,
Hamlet

Cats and monkeys,
monkeys and cats –
all human life is there.
*Henry James, **The***
Madonna of the Future

At that time I possessed a very pretty small tortoise called Mary Ann. Thomas Henry, my cat, was devoted to her. They used to drink milk out of the same saucer, and when they had finished, Thomas Henry would lick the milk off Mary Ann's head and neck, and tidy her up generally.

Rev J. G. Wood, **Petland Revisited**

'What a beautiful cat!' exclaims your guest.
If you are unwise in the ways of cats, you will
commit the indiscretion of calling the cat to you.
There is an awkward pause, while your cat
reflectively examines a dainty paw, or a table leg.
Foolishly, you call again. Your cat looks in the
opposite direction, yawns gracefully and strolls
off with an air of complete unconcern.

Michael Joseph, **Cat's Company**

Cats are a very nice animal in some ways.
I don't have a cat but I would like a dog.

Bella, **6**

Cats can be very funny, and have the oddest
ways of showing they're glad to see you.
Rudimace always peed in our shoes.

W.H. Auden

Dogs come when they are called; cats take
a message and get back to you.

Mary Bly

There are no ordinary cats.

Colette

Only cat lovers know the luxury of fur-coated,
musical hot water bottles that never go cold.

Susanne Millen

Long contact with the human race has developed
in [the cat] the art of diplomacy, and no Roman
Cardinal of medieval days knew better how to
ingratiate himself with his surroundings than a
cat with a saucer of cream on its mental horizon.

Saki, **The Achievement of the Cat**

My cat can talk. I asked her what two
minus two was and she said nothing.

Traditional

Mr Lunardi, who made a journey in a hot
air balloon on 15 September 1784, was
accompanied in his aerial passage by a couple
of pigeons, a cat and a favourite lap-dog.

Cats do not wear their hearts on their sleeves,
which is not to say that they do not miss you
when you are away. However, they feel that
you have behaved very badly and may not be
very civil when you return. After you have
apologized, normal relations can be resumed.

Susanne Millen

The fat cat on the mat
may seem to dream
of nice mice that suffice
for him, or cream;
but he is free, maybe,
walks in thought
unbowed, proud, where loud
roared and fought
his kin, lean and slim,
or deep in den
in the East feasted on beasts
and tender men.

J.R.R. Tolkein, **The Adventures of**
Tom Bombadil

I think cats are pests because they try
and eat my pet frogs.

Jonathan, **6**

My cat is called Boots. My cat chases mice all over the house. My cat sleeps on the sofa. My cat is very, very naughty.

Emma, 7

A cat isn't fussy - just so long as you remember he likes his milk in the shallow, rose-patterned saucer and his fish on the blue plate. From which he will take it, and eat it off the floor.

Arthur Bridges

Cats only assume their strangest, most intriguing and most beautiful postures when it is impossible to photograph them. Cat calendars always disappoint for they only show the public range of cat positions.

J.R. Coulson

I love Mozart the cat next door.

James, 7

If your cat falls out of a tree,
go indoors to laugh.

Patricia Hitchcock

French novelist Colette was a firm cat-lover.
When she was in the US she saw a cat sitting in
the street. She went over to talk to it and the
two of them mewed at each other for a friendly
minute. Colette turned to her companion and
exclaimed, 'Enfin! Quelqu'un qui parle français.'
(At last! Someone who speaks French.)

Anonymous

My mum likes cats. So do I. But the
worst thing about cats is they smell.

Sophie, 7

Any cat who misses a mouse pretends
it was aiming for the dead leaf.
Charlotte Gray

I saw a Puritan-one,
Hanging of his cat on Monday,
For killing of a mouse on Sunday.
Richard Braithwaite, **Barnabee's Journal**

He has gone to fish for his Aunt Jobiska's
Runcible Cat with crimson whiskers!
Edward Lear, **Nonsense Songs**

I would like to be there, were it
but to see how the cat jumps.
Sir Walter Scott

Tailless cats are a reminder that, according to legend, the pair of cats due to enter the Ark were late. Noah was just closing the door and in doing so nipped off their tails.

Traditional legend

Cats, no less liquid than their shadows,
  Offer no angles to the wind.
They slip, diminished, neat, through
  loopholes less than themselves.

A.S.J. Tessimond, **Cats II**

Cats have had their goose,
  Cooked by tobacco juice;
Still why deny its use ...?

C.S. Calverley, **Ode to Tobacco**

It (the Cheshire Cat) vanished quite
slowly, beginning with the end of the tail,
and ending with the grin, which remained
some time after the rest had gone.
Lewis Carroll, **Alice in Wonderland**

I do not like cats because they
scratch me all the time.
Ronak, 7

'Is it bad luck to have a black cat following you?'
'Well, it depends on whether you're a
man or a mouse.'

The great open spaces
Where cats are cats.
Don Marquis, **Mehitabel has an adventure**

The greater cats with golden eyes
Stare out between the bars.
Deserts are there, and different skies
And night with different stars.
Vita Sackville-West

When the cat is abroad, the mice play.
*John Florio, **First Fruites***

Within that porch, across the way,
I see two naked eyes this night;
Two eyes that neither shut nor blink,
Searching my face with a green light.
But cats to me are strange, so strange
I cannot sleep if one is near;
And though I'm sure I see those eyes,
I'm not so sure a body's there!
W.H. Davies

A cat is an animal that never cries
over spilled milk.

Proverb

Poets generally love cats - because poets have
no delusions about their own superiority.

Marion Garretty

Most cats, when they are out want to be in,
and vice versa, and often simultaneously.

Dr Louis J. Camuti

Careful observers may foretell the hour
(By sure prognostics) when to dread a shower;
While rain depends, the pensive cat gives o'er
Her frolics, and pursues her tail no more.

Jonathan Swift

A halfpenny cat may look like a king.
*John Ray, **Scottish Proverbs***

•

I have a cat and he has diabetes, but I love him.
*Andrew, **6***

•

The lion and his tamer
They had a little tiff,
For the lion limped too lamely,
The bars had bored him stiff.

No call to crack your whip, Sir!

Said the lion then, irate:
No need to snap my head off,
Said the tamer - but too late.
*Gerda Mayer, **The Crunch***

I fed some lemon to a cat and got a sour puss.
Traditional joke

As to sagacity, I should say that his judgment respecting the warmest place and the softest cushion in a room is infallible, his punctuality at meal times is admirable, and his pertinacity in jumping on people's shoulders till they give him some of the best of what is going, indicates great firmness.

Thomas Henry Huxley

Whenever he was out of luck and a little down-hearted, he would fall to mourning over the loss of a wonderful cat he used to own (for where women and children are not, men of kindly impulses take up with pets, for they must love something) ...

Mark Twain, **Dick Baker's Cat**

Cats make an impression on us which we fortify and elaborate with our own imaginations. It is no crime and we love them all the more because of it.

Lloyd Alexander, **Heathcliff**

The Cat will kill mice, and he will be kind to babies when he is in the house, just so long as they do not pull his tail too hard. But when he has done that, and between times, and when the moon gets up and night comes, he is the Cat that walks by himself, and all places are alike to him. Then he goes out to the Wet Wild Woods or up on the Wet Wild Trees or on the Wet Wild Roofs, waving his wild tail and walking by his wild lone.

Rudyard Kipling, **The Cat Who Walked by Himself**

... for Mrs Miller, though she was indeed a fat slut and had no beauty and few virtues, felt strongly enough about cats to get out of her bed an hour or more early two days a week, winter, and summer; and no other passion she was capable of had anything but the opposite effect.

Margaret Bonham, **A Fine Place for the Cat**

Kiss the black cat,

An' twill make ye fat;

Kiss the white ane,

'Twill make ye lean.

English folk rhyme

The cat and dog may kiss,

yet are none the better friends.

Bohn

A cat has nine lives - 'It was permitted for

a witch to take her cattes body nine times.'

Baldwin, **Beware the Cat**

Diddlety, diddlety, dumpty,

The cat ran up a plum tree;

Half a crown

To fetch her down,

Diddlety, diddlety, dumpty.

Old English nursery rhyme

Mrs Crupp had indignantly assured him that there wasn't room to swing a cat there; but as Mr Dick justly observed to me, sitting down on the foot of the bed, nursing his leg, 'You know, Trotwood, I don't want to swing a cat. I never do swing a cat. Therefore what does that signify to me.'

*Charles Dickens, **David Copperfield***

As busy as a cat in a tripe shop.

*J.D. Robertson, **Gloucester Gloss***

He that will play with a cat, must expect
to be scratched.

S. Palmer, **Moral Essays on Proverbs**

What female heart can gold despise?
What cat's averse to fish?
Thomas Gray, **Ode on the Death of a Favourite Cat**

Cat! who hast pass'd thy grand climacteric,
How many mice and rats has in thy days
Destroy'd? – How many titbits stolen? Gaze
  With those bright languid segments
    green, and prick
Those velvet ears – but pr'ythee do not stick
  Thy great talons in me – and upraise
  Thy gentle mew – and tell me all thy frays
Of fish and mice, and rats and tender chick.
Nay, look not down, nor lick thy dainty wrists –
  For all the wheezy asthma, – and for all
Thy tail's tip is nick'd off – and though the fists
Of many a maid have given thee many a maul,
  Still is that fur as soft as when the lists
In youth thou ener'dst on glass-bottled wall.

John Keats

Acknowledgements:

The Publishers wish to thank everyone who gave permission to reproduce the quotes in this book. Every effort has been made to contact the copyright holders, but in the event that an oversight has occurred, the publishers would be delighted to rectify any omissions in future editions of this book. Children's quotes supplied courtesy of Herne Hill School; *Jennie*, Paul Gallico, reprinted courtesy of Souvenir Press; *Cat's Company*, Michael Joseph, reprinted courtesy of Michael Joseph, a division of Penguin Books; W. H. Auden, Faber & Faber; *The Adventures of Tom Bambadil*, J.R.R. Tolkein, reprinted courtesy of Unwin Hyman, a division of HarperCollins; *Cats*, A.S.J. Tessimond, reprinted courtesy of University of Reading, on behalf of Hubert Nicholson; Jenny de Vries, Charlotte Gray, Roseanne Ambrose Brown and Susanne Millen extracts from *Cat Quotations*, 1991; *The Cat Who Walked by Himself*, Rudyard Kipling, reprinted courtesy of Macmillan Publishers; *Heathcliffe*, from *Quorum of Cats* by Lloyd Alexander, reproduced by permission of A.M. Heath & Company Ltd; *A Fine Place for a Cat*, Margaret Bonham, reprinted courtesy of Curtis Brown Ltd.